First Questions and Answers about **How Things Work**

Why Do Balls Bounce?

TIME
LIFE *for*
Children®

ALEXANDRIA, VIRGINIA

Contents

Why does toast pop up?

Because it is hot. A toaster starts working when someone puts a slice of bread into it and pushes down on the handle. Inside the toaster, thin wires get very, very hot. They toast the bread until it is brown and crispy.

At the same time, a switch inside the toaster gets hot, too. When the switch gets hot enough, it turns the toaster off and makes your toast pop up.

It's toasty in here!

4

How does a stove cook my oatmeal?

Stoves make heat to cook food. Some stoves burn gas for heat; others use electricity to heat metal coils. Inside gas stoves are metal tubes. When someone turns a dial on the stove, gas flows out of the tube to a burner. Then a tiny flame or a spark makes the gas catch fire, cooking your oatmeal.

Electric stoves have metal burners. Electricity going through the metal makes them hot. These burners heat up more slowly than gas burners, but they stay hot for a long time after the electricity is turned off.

6

Let's look inside the burner!

7

How does a refrigerator keep my juice cold?

A refrigerator takes heat away so things inside it stay cold. It has long, thin pipes that start inside its walls and go out the back. A liquid called refrigerant flows through the pipes.

Inside the pipes, the liquid turns into a gas, soaking up the heat inside the refrigerator. Everything inside the refrigerator, including your juice, stays cool. Then the gas turns back into a liquid and starts through the pipes again.

9

How does water come out of the faucet?

A faucet handle is connected to a small, round piece of rubber underneath it called a washer. The washer stops water from flowing through the water pipe and out the spout.

When you turn the handle, the washer moves up a bit. Now the water flows past it and out the faucet's spout. When you turn the handle the other way, you put the washer back in place and the water stops.

Did you know?

If a faucet leaks, it often means a washer is worn out. A little water is slipping through the washer and dripping out the spout.

11

How can I hear my friend on the telephone?

When your friend speaks into a telephone, the sound of his voice is turned into an electrical signal. It travels from his house to your house through the air or through wires. Then your telephone turns the signal back into sound and you hear his voice.

Try it!
Take two paper cups. Poke a hole in the bottom of each cup and run a long piece of string from one cup to the other. To keep the string in place, tie each end to half of a toothpick inside the cups. Now pull the string tight. Put one cup to your ear. Have someone speak into the other cup. Can you hear a voice?

13

How does a key open a lock?

A lock has a middle part called a barrel. Several small metal pins stick into the barrel and keep it from turning.

A key has a lot of uneven bumps on its side. When you slide the right key into the lock, each bump pushes a metal pin out of the way. Now the key can turn this barrel. As it turns, the lock springs open.

You can't open a lock with the wrong key. Its bumps won't line up to push the pins just the right distance.

How does a bicycle work?

The muscles in your legs help to make your bike go. As you push down on the pedals, one thing leads to another:

3. The chain turns another gear attached to the back wheel. Because it is smaller, this gear turns even faster. It makes the back wheel turn, and that pushes your bike forward.

1. The pedals are attached to a metal wheel with teeth on it called a gear. This gear turns with the pedals.

2. A chain fits around the outside of the gear. As the gear moves, it turns the chain.

17

How do traffic lights change from red to green?

Some traffic lights are run by special clocks called timers. After the red light is on for a certain amount of time, the timer switches to the green light. The timer switches the lights on and off all day and night.

Other lights work in a different way. Something called a sensor under the street keeps track of the cars that stop at the light. When the cars have waited long enough, the sensor switches the light from red to green.

Did you know?

At some corners there are buttons for people who want to cross the street. A person pushes the button and the traffic light stops the cars when it is time to walk.

How do pens write?

In the center of most pens is a long tube filled with ink. The ink moves through the tube to a tiny metal ball at the pen's tip. As you write or draw, the ball rolls over your paper, spreading ink as it goes. These pens are called ballpoint pens.

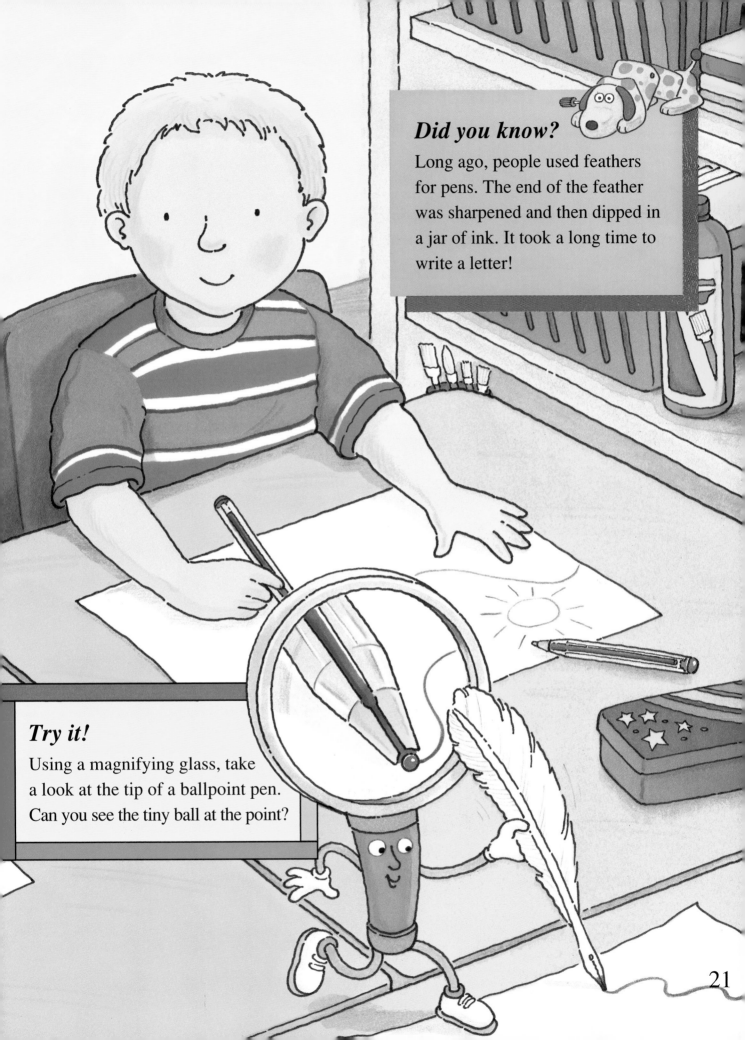

Did you know?

Long ago, people used feathers for pens. The end of the feather was sharpened and then dipped in a jar of ink. It took a long time to write a letter!

Try it!

Using a magnifying glass, take a look at the tip of a ballpoint pen. Can you see the tiny ball at the point?

21

Where do pencil marks go when you erase them?

Pencil marks are a little sticky. When you rub them with an eraser, the marks cling to it. The eraser also scratches away some of the paper. After you finish erasing, you brush away tiny broken bits of eraser and paper, and the pencil marks go with them.

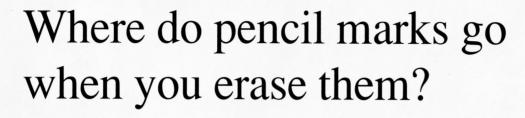

Try it!

Make a pencil mark on a piece of paper. Cover part of it with clear tape. Rub the tape with your finger. Now lift the tape off the paper. Did some of that sticky pencil mark go with it?

What makes a wind-up toy go?

A wind-up toy has a spring inside. This tiny coil of wire gets tighter and tighter as you wind it. When you let go, the spring goes back to the way it was. As it unwinds, it turns gears. The turning gears make the toy move forward—or crawl sideways—or even jump up in the air!

24

Why do balls bounce?

Because they are made of stretchy stuff called rubber. When a rubber ball hits the ground, it flattens out a little on the bottom. When the rubber snaps back to its round shape, the ball bounces.

Did you know?

Rubber bands work the same way. When you pull on one, the rubber *s-t-r-e-t-c-h-e-s*. When you let go, it snaps back to its regular shape.

26

Why do binoculars make things look bigger?

Binoculars have curved pieces of glass or plastic called lenses. When light goes through the lenses, it bends, and whatever you're looking at seems bigger. Through binoculars, something far away looks very close.

Try it!
Lenses can also make things seem smaller than they really are. Turn your binoculars around and look at something through the wrong end. How do things look?

I'm a lens, too!

29

How can doors open by themselves?

Some doors, such as those in stores or airports, have ways of sensing when someone is coming toward them. Above the doors is an electric box that sends out invisible waves through the air. These waves bounce off anything that moves toward the door and then return to the box. The box then sends an electric signal to the door to open.

How does a radio make music?

It picks it up from the air! The music begins at a radio station far away. At the station, the music is turned into signals. These signals leave the radio station in all directions. They fly through the air in tiny waves that we can't see, touch, or hear.

A radio has a piece of wire or metal called an antenna. It catches the signals. Then the radio turns them back into sounds we can hear.

Did you know?

Many radio stations send out signals, but a radio can play only one signal at a time. As you turn the dial on the radio, you choose the signal you want to hear.

33

How do pictures show up on my television?

Televisions work a lot like radios. They pick up signals from TV stations far away. Then they turn them into sound and pictures.

The part of the television set that you watch is called the picture tube. Inside the tube, a special kind of gun shoots electricity at the screen. This causes many, many dots on the TV screen to light up. When all those dots light up together, they make the picture you see.

Did you know?
With cable TV, the electrical signals travel to the set through wires instead of through the air.

35

Where do escalator steps go?

At the top of an escalator that's going down, the steps seem to come out of the floor. At the bottom the steps seem to disappear.

That's because the escalator is a big moving circle of stairs. Under the escalator are turning gears that make a chain move. The escalator's steps are attached to the chain. So as long as the chain moves, the steps go around and around and up and down.

Why do pinwheels spin?

Because air pushes on their blades! Every wheel needs something to make it turn, and a pinwheel needs the moving air we call wind. As you blow on the pinwheel, the air pushes one cuplike blade after another and the pinwheel spins.

39

Why do rubber ducks squeak?

Because you squeeze air out of them! Squeaky toys are filled with air. When you squeeze one, you push all the air out a tiny hole. The air makes the edges of the hole move very quickly. Those quick little moves make the sound our ears hear.

Try it!

Hold your fingertips near the hole in your favorite squeaky toy.

Now squeeze hard with your other hand. Can your fingers feel the air rushing out the hole?

41

How do toilets flush?

To flush a toilet, you press a small handle. The handle lifts a rubber stopper inside the tank, which is filled with clean water. When the stopper lifts up, the water rushes through a pipe from the tank into the toilet bowl. The swirling water carries everything down the drain.

When the tank is empty, the stopper blocks the pipe again. Then more clean water fills the tank.

Try it!
Ask a grownup to take the lid off the toilet tank. Can you see the stopper and other parts inside?

How do light bulbs make light?

They use electricity. Electricity travels through wires in the walls to the plug and then into the bulb. Inside the bulb, the electricity goes through a special wire called a filament. When that happens, the filament gets so hot that it glows brightly. That glow lights up the bulb.

Try it!

The next time a light bulb burns out, ask a grownup to show it to you. Hold the bulb near your ear and shake it. That tiny piece you hear inside is the filament, which broke when the light burned out.

45

How does a light switch work?

The switch is connected to wires in your walls that carry electricity. When you flip a switch on, you make the wires touch. The electricity flows all the way to the light and turns it on. When you flip a switch off, the wires come apart. Since the electricity can't go through the wires to the light, the light turns off.

46

Did you know?
Some night-lights have a kind of switch that turns on by itself whenever the room gets dark.

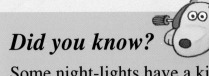

TIME-LIFE for CHILDREN®

Managing Editor: Patricia Daniels
Editorial Directors: Jean Burke Crawford, Allan Fallow,
Karin Kinney, Sara Mark
Senior Art Director: Susan K. White
Publishing Associate: Marike van der Veen
Editorial Assistant: Mary Saxton
Production Manager: Marlene Zack
Senior Copyeditor: Colette Stockum
Quality Assurance Manager: Miriam Newton
Library: Louise D. Forstall, Anne Heising

Special Contributor: Barbara Klein
Writer: Andrew Gutelle

Designed by: David Bennett Books

Series design: David Bennett
Book design: David Bennett
Art direction: David Bennett
Illustrated by: Steve Cox
Additional cover
 illustrations by: Nick Baxter

First printing. Printed in U.S.A.
Published simultaneously in Canada.

Time Life Inc. is a wholly owned subsidiary of THE TIME INC. BOOK COMPANY.

TIME-LIFE is a trademark of Time Warner Inc. U.S.A.
For subscription information, call 1-800-621-7026.

School and library distribution by Time-Life Education, P.O. Box 85026, Richmond, VA 23285-5026

Library of Congress Cataloging-in-Publication Data

Why do balls bounce? : first questions and answers about how things work.
p. cm.—(Time-Life Library of first questions and answers)
ISBN 0-7835-0901-4.
1. Science—Miscellanea—Juvenile literature. 2. Engineering—Miscellanea—Juvenile literature. 3. Science—Study and teaching (Elementary)—Activity programs. 4. Engineering—Study and teaching (Elementary)—Activity programs.
[1. Technology—Miscellanea. 2. Science—Miscellanea. 3. Questions and answers.]
I. Time-Life for Children (Firm) II. Series: Library of first questions and answers.
Q163.W4924 1995
95-3746

620—dc20
CIP

Consultants

Dr. Lewis P. Lipsitt, an internationally recognized specialist on childhood development, was the 1990 recipient of the Nicholas Hobbs Award for science in the service of children. He has served as the science director for the American Psychological Association and is a professor of psychology and medical science at Brown University, where he directed the Child Study Center for 25 years.

Andrew Pogan is a high-school teacher of chemistry and physics in Montgomery County, Maryland.

Dr. Judith A. Schickedanz, an authority on the education of preschool children, is an associate professor of early childhood education at the Boston University School of Education, where she also directs the Early Childhood Learning Laboratory. Her published work includes *More Than the ABCs: Early Stages of Reading and Writing Development* as well as several textbooks and many scholarly papers.